L I

P

JEFF SHORT

LIFE'S LITTLE PLEASURES

JEFF SHORT

First Published in 1998
by Jarrold Publishing, Whitefriars,
Norwich NR3 1TR

ISBN 0-7117-1053-8

Printed in Great Britain 1/98

People tell me that I'm always smiling, and although that's not strictly true, I have found that the best way to survive the trials and tribulations that life can bring is to remind myself from time to time just how good it can be.

To help others do the same, I've compiled this book of little pleasures. Dip into it anywhere and you'll find something that will bring a smile to your face and give you a warm glow of recognition.

A dew covered cobweb glistening in the sunlight.

Toasting crumpets on a log fire on a wet winter afternoon.

The smell of bacon cooking.

Finding lots of letters on your doormat and not one of them a bill.

Breakfast in bed.

Completing the Times crossword.

Someone else washing your car.

Reading your old school reports.

Comfort eating with a like-minded friend.

Bumping into an old friend you haven't seen for years.

The colours of autumn.

Receiving flowers on your birthday.

Receiving flowers for no reason at all.

Stroking someone's head when they've just had a very short haircut.

Splashing through puddles
in your welly boots.

A long, slow stroll in the country.

Watching new-born lambs
take their first steps.

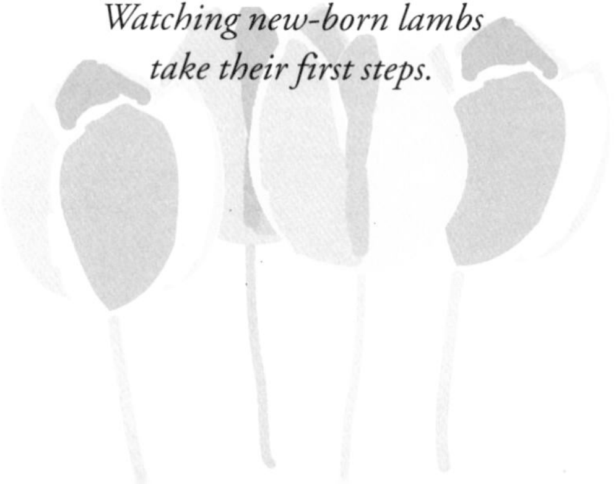

Waking up and thinking you have to go to work, then remembering that it's Saturday.

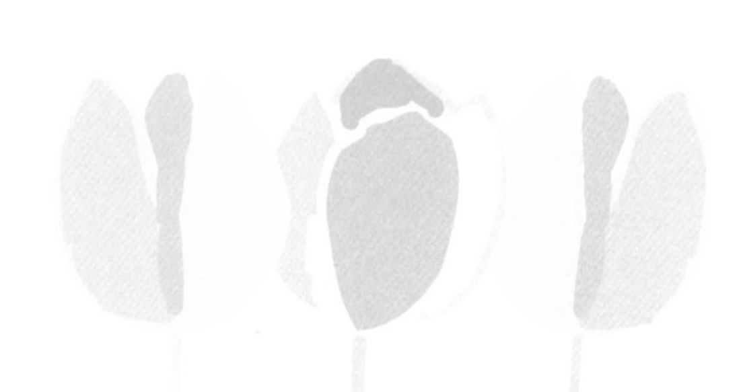

Shopping with your best friend.

Browsing in junk shops.

Managing to open a milk carton without spilling it.

Flipping your fried egg without breaking the yolk.

Winning at Scrabble, without the aid of a dictionary.

Being told by your dentist that you don't need any fillings.

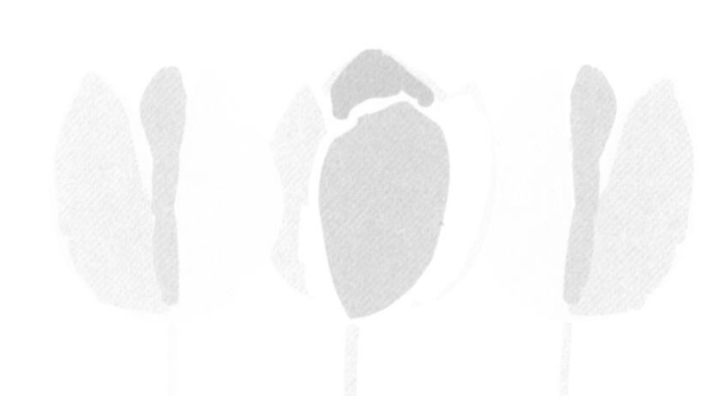

Being offered a job you really want.

Being offered a job you don't want.

Lying in a hammock,
sipping a drink.

Bees buzzing on a summer day.

Water trickling through your toes on the seashore.

Cooking the first home grown vegetables of the year.

Feeding ducks.

Playing 'Pooh Sticks'.

The smell of honeysuckle.

Finally managing to light the barbecue.

Warm rain in the middle of a dry summer.

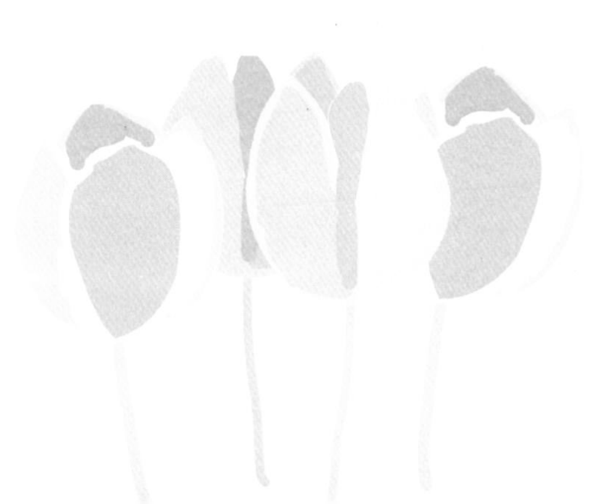

Popping the bubbles on bubble wrap.

Bursting balloons.

Finding money in the pocket of an old coat.

Finding money down the back of the sofa.

The feel of velvet.

The smell of baking bread.

Watching a nursery school nativity play.

Sunday breakfast in your favourite café.

The first time the baby sleeps through the night.

Walking in the rain.

Listening to New Orleans jazz bands.

Battered but much loved teddy bears.

Someone reading to you at bedtime.

Receiving more than one Valentine card.

Receiving a Valentine card and really not knowing who sent it.

Laughing until it hurts.

Being given a hug.

Singing along to the car radio, very loudly and out-of-tune.

Listening to a storm raging when you're warm and cosy indoors.

Watching puppies playing.

Curling up in your favourite armchair.

The slow tick-tock of a grandfather clock.

The relief of a good scratch.

Having the wind behind you on a long bike ride.

Finding the TV remote control.

Possession of the TV remote control.

Trying a new recipe and the finished result looking just like the photo in the book.

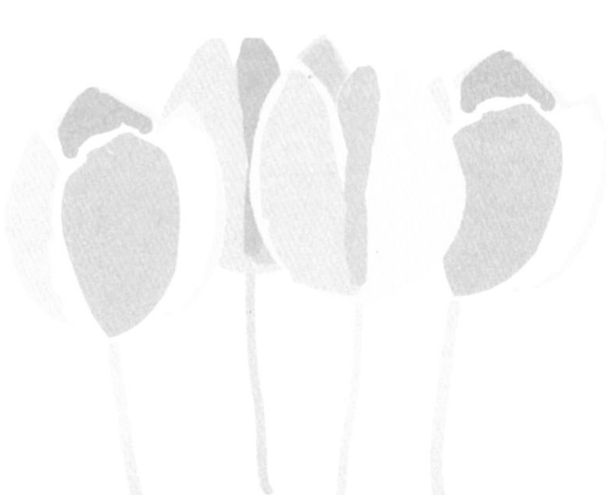

Kicking through a pile of leaves.

Still, frosty mornings.

Putting the last piece into a jigsaw puzzle.

Losing weight when you haven't been trying.

A traditional British pub.

Watching a fireworks display.

Thatched cottages with roses round the door.

Strawberries and cream on a balmy summer evening.

Sitting on the bank of a crystal clear stream.

Dragonflies shimmering in the sunlight.

A spectacular sunset.

Trying something new and finding you like it.

Unsolicited compliments.

Buying ten CDs at once and not giving a second thought to your credit card bill.

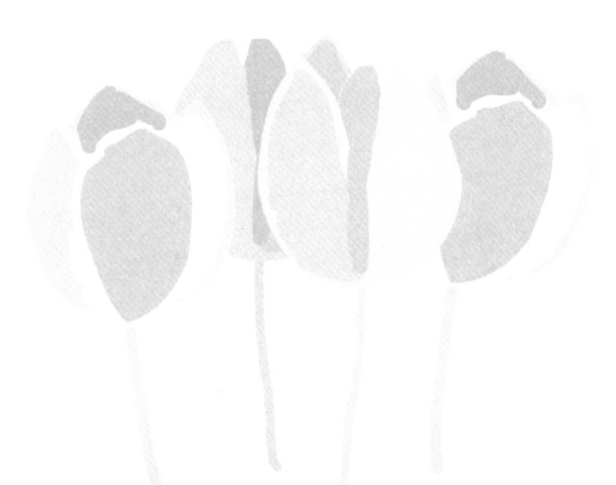

Chocolate.

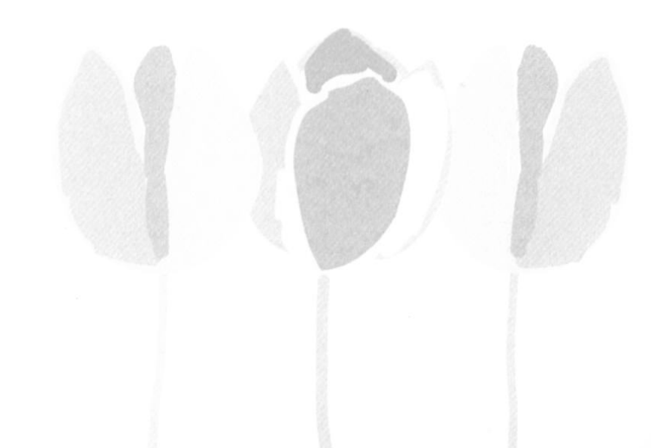

Giving in to temptation – there's no virtue in virtue!

Cool cotton sheets on a
hot summer night.

Flying a kite on top of a hill.

Building sandcastles.

The smell of freshly roasting coffee beans.

Four hours in a bookshop.

Watching a field of corn sway in the breeze.

Eating popcorn at the movies.

Making new friends.

Stepping on to dry land after a rough ferry crossing.

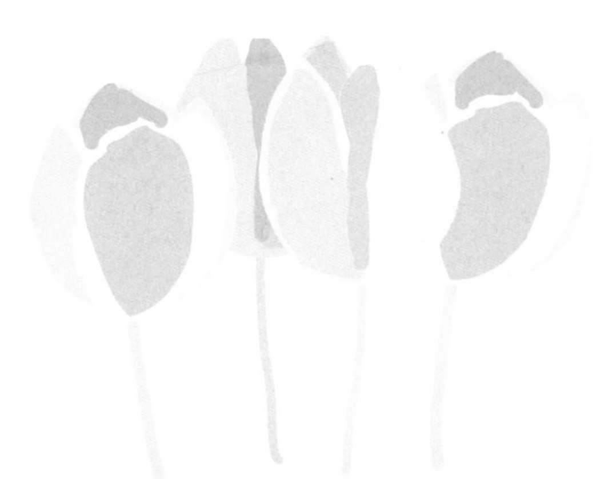

Waking up to the silence that follows
a heavy snowfall.

First love.

Nostalgia.

Building a bonfire and then watching it burn.

Soaking your feet after a long walk.

Climbing in your own bed after having been away.

Getting the keys to your first house.

Spotting a speed trap.

Finding an unexpected bargain.

Walking the dog before work.

Knowing the way when asked directions.

The smell of a forest in autumn.

Thinking of other people at work while you're on holiday.

Managing not to kill your house plants.

Managing not to kill somebody else's house plants.

Receiving an unexpected tax rebate.

Choosing the quickest moving queue.

Being told that your car doesn't need repairs.

The day your puppy is finally house-trained.

Watching a bird feeding its young.

The smell of freshly cut grass.

A full English breakfast.

Bluebell woods in spring.

Watching a child sleeping.

Two tickets to Paris.

Decorating a Christmas tree.

Finding a new hairstyle.

Having a good yawn and stretch.

Meeting someone at a railway station.

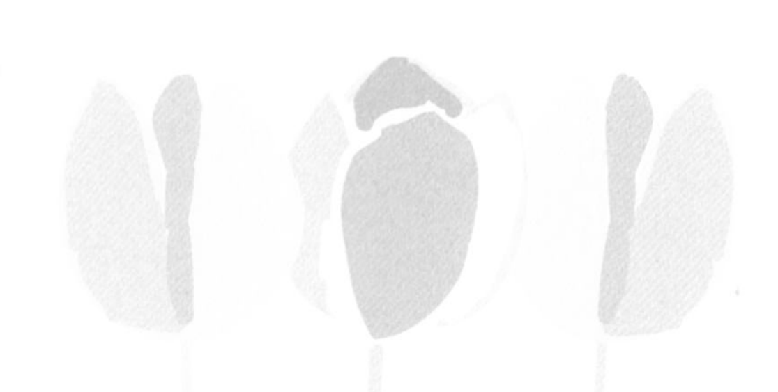

Having a pizza delivered.

Not answering a ringing telephone.

Tall ships in full sail.

Making a snowman.

Enjoying a good meal with friends.

A crowded candle-lit Christmas carol service in a small church.

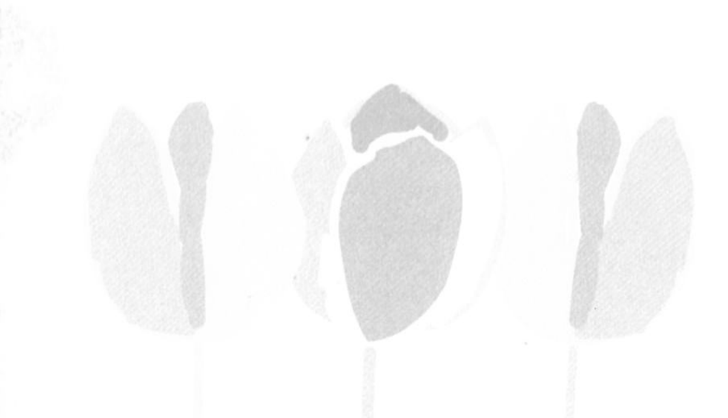

Being welcomed home by your children.

Putting on warm pyjamas after a hot bath.

Reading a book that you really can't put down.

Reading a book that makes you laugh out loud.

The car starting first time on a frosty morning.

Somebody emptying the vacuum cleaner for you.

When the wallpaper looks as good on the wall as it did in the catalogue.

Watching a movie with a happy ending.

Picnics in the park.

Seeing a butterfly
dance on the breeze.

Getting back your holiday photos.

Discovering a new restaurant.

Being wrapped up nice and warm on a bitterly cold day.

Finding the secret level on your new computer game.

The smell of freshly sawn wood.

The sound of waves against pebbles.

Seeing a brilliant rainbow.

Looking for a face in the clouds.

Knowing it's not your turn to take out the garbage.

Choosing what to buy with a gift token.

Passing your driving test.

Finishing a big pile of ironing.

Getting the auto-timer on your cooker to work.

Finding your glasses.

Listening to the dawn chorus.

Being given the day off work without asking.

Out-smarting your boss.

Knowing that it's someone else's turn
to do the washing-up.

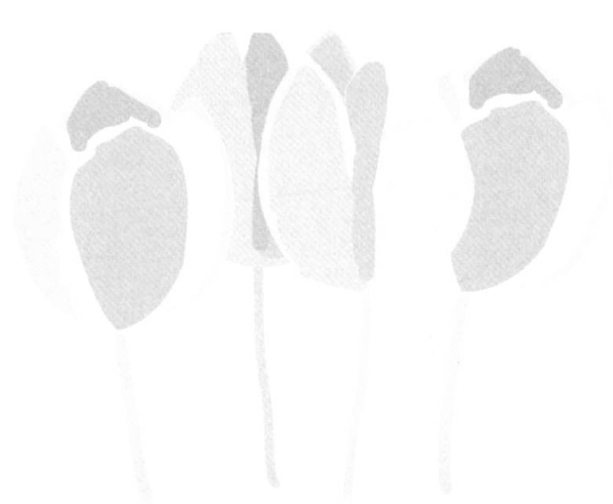

The crackle and smell of a bonfire.

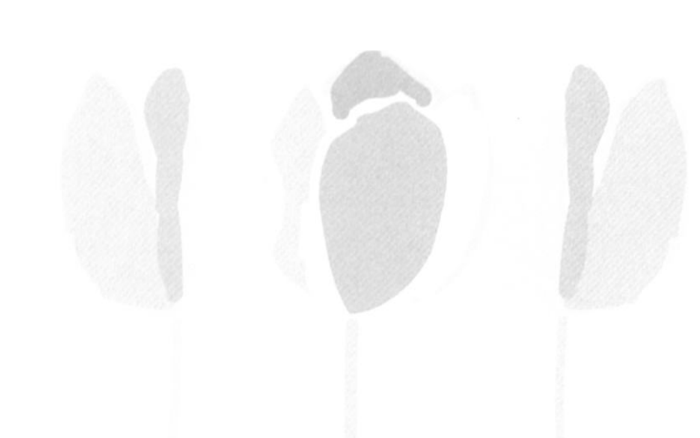

Finding the perfect birthday gift.

Receiving the perfect birthday gift.

Watching a swan land on water.

Paddling in the sea.

Looking at brilliant stars in a dark sky.

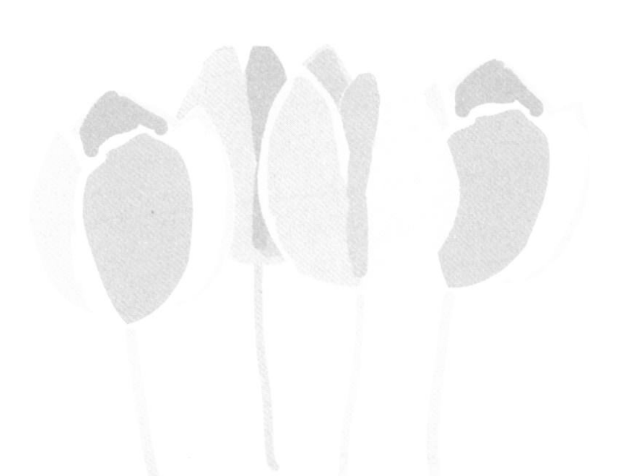

Someone else cooking the dinner.

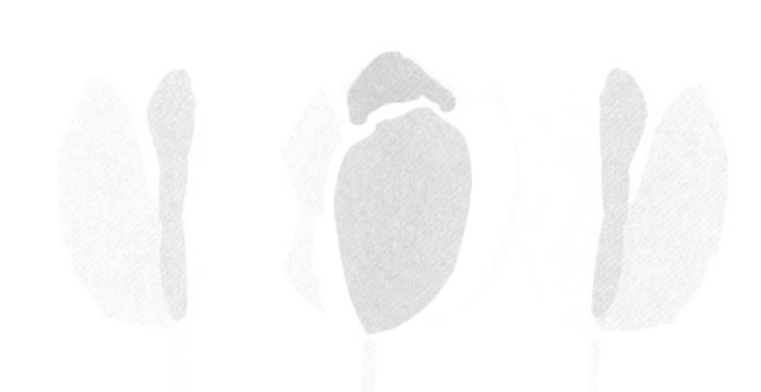

Reading bedtime stories to children.

A traditional Sunday lunch.

Not being overdrawn at Christmas.

Emptying your in-tray.

A hot water bottle on a chilly night.

Having a table to yourself on a long train journey.

Your train actually arriving on time.

Finding something you thought you had lost.

Walking on a deserted beach in a winter storm.

Having a bath run for you.

Finding the other sock.

Understanding why your computer has crashed.

Finishing exams.

Not running out of food at a dinner party.

Finally finishing the decorating.

Finding clothes that actually fit.

Watching a traffic jam when you're on a train.

Cream tea in a country tea shop.

Picking your own fruit.

A really good jumble sale.

Your last day at school.

The sun shining on your birthday.

Hearing the rapid spitting of frying food.

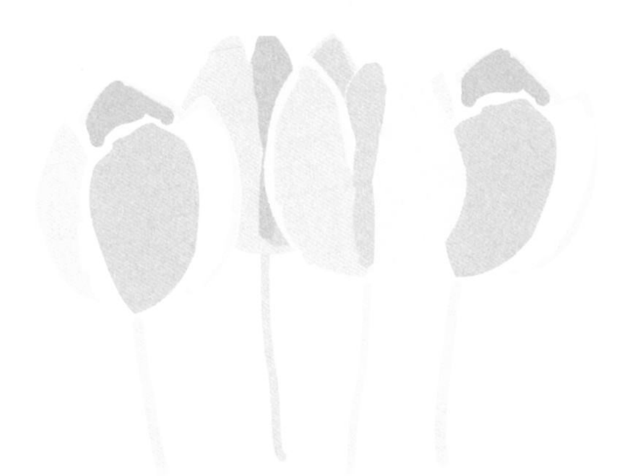

Making the first footprints in fresh snow.

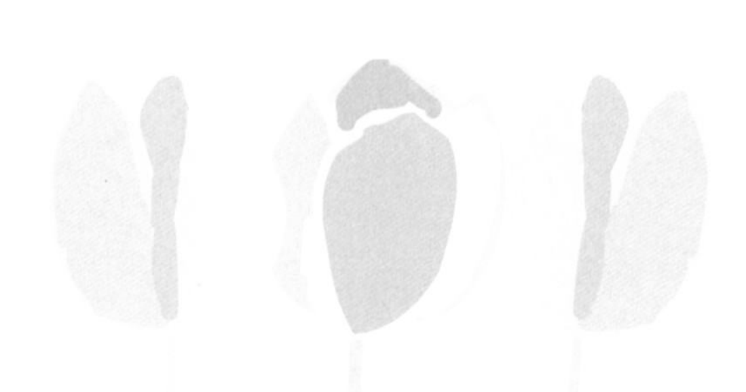

Having a lie-in on a Sunday.

Going back to bed with a cup of tea.

Dappled sunlight in a beech wood.

The smell of apples.

The scent of flowers on a summer evening.

A dewdrop sparkling on a rose petal.

Having your first book published.